This book is due for return on or before the last date shown
above; it may, subject to the book not being reserved by
another reader, be renewed by personal application, post, or
telephone, quoting this date and details of the book.

HAMPSHIRE COUNTY LIBRARY

Winchester
~o~
Seen and Remembered

Philippa Stevens & Derek Dine

Cover and title page : King Alfred statue in the Broadway, Winchester.

Hampshire County Library

Copyright © 1978 Hampshire County Library

ISBN 0 901406 02 3

Printed in Great Britain by Bradley and Son Limited
50–56 Portman Road, Reading, RG3 1EY

50 11

Introduction
The photographs on the following pages illustrate the changing face of Winchester by comparing street scenes of different dates. The authors have selected views of the city area, the furthest location being St. Cross. Some of the photographs date from the last century, some from about the turn of the century and others from the 1920s and 1930s. Some are from the County Library's own photographic collection and others are reproduced from the County Museum Service and County Record Office collections.

Acknowledgements
The authors wish to thank the following institutions for permission to reproduce old photographs: Hampshire County Museum Service (pages 25 and 35) Hampshire Record Office (pages 1, 11, 21, 23, 27, 33 and 37) and Hampshire Field Club and Archaeological Society (pages 9, 15, 29, 31, 39 and 41).
Thanks are also due to John Woodhead, the County Library Design and Display Officer, who is responsible for the layout and design of this publication.

Notes on the authors
Derek Dine is Divisional Librarian of the Central Division of Hampshire County Library. He has been based at Winchester for many years, is a keen amateur photographer and has taken all the modern photographs within the last two years. Philippa Stevens is the Local History Librarian of Hampshire County Library and is also based at Winchester. She has lived and worked in the city for over ten years, first as a reference librarian and latterly with local history specialisation.

The George Hotel
This famous inn was photographed in the 1930s before traffic lights controlled the High Street junction. An inn stood on this site in 1408 and was called The Moon until the Battle of Agincourt (1415) when it was renamed The George after King Henry's battlecry.

1

Southgate Corner

The George Hotel was demolished in 1956 when the junction of Jewry Street was widenend. A building of similar proportions was designed for Barclay's Bank, and opened in 1959. The rounded corner of Southgate Street was known for decades as Hayward's Corner.

Jewry Street c. 1920
The old building seen before restoration has been the property of St. John's Hospital for centuries. The square-fronted building beyond was the Golden Lion Inn before it lost its licence in 1907 and became a butcher's shop. The hand-cart is parked outside a grocer's shop.

3

Jewry Street

The restoration of the buildings in the 1920s revealed their true period, and the modern restaurant is called The Elizabethan in honour of their antiquity. The grocer's shop is still carried on at no. 16 although under a different name, and a building society completes the architectural group.

St. George's Street
Often mentioned as a back lane in old documents, St. George's Street
remained much the same for centuries. The street acted as a service-road
for shops which fronted onto High Street, and its many industrial buildings
included workshops, factories, warehouses and a couple of slaughterhouses.

St. George's Street
The road-widening of 1956–57 left few buildings untouched, but the
Masonic Hall remains much the same. All the factories were moved out to
the newly-created Winnall Industrial Estate by the early 1960s. The Casson
Block was built in 1962–65 to designs by Casson, Conder and Partners.

High Street looking east
The photographer caught the sunshine on a showery day for this view of
High Street about the turn of the century. The building with the shuttered
windows on the extreme left is the George Hotel, and almost opposite are
the offices of the Hampshire Chronicle.

High Street looking east
The George Hotel has given way to Barclay's Bank but the Hampshire Chronicle
offices remain unchanged save for the improvement of the window-boxes.
The building immediately beyond was a cinema for many years, but is now
used by Courts the furnishers.

The King's Head Inn
The King's Head stood at 17 Little Minster Street and dated back to about 1660 or earlier. It was a charming old inn and had a picturesque yard at the back. The next but one property was the Winchester Temperance Billiards Hall for many years.

Little Minster Street
The King's Head was demolished in 1936 and the billiards hall became the
United Services' Club during wartime. In the later 1950s the building was
used as a chocolate factory, closing down in 1966. The building is now the
headquarters of the Winchester Archaeological Rescue Group.

High Street from City Cross c. 1929
The Norman Palace Tea Rooms occupied the approximate site of the old
royal palace used by the Saxon and Norman kings before the castle was
built. The town pump used to stand near the site of the pillar box but was
removed last century as the water became foul.

High Street looking west
This spacious view shows the upper end of the pedestrian precinct, and
demonstrates how little the buildings have changed. The bank was built
about 1780 near the site of the Chequers Inn. It now sports mirror-glass in
the windows, but what a pity the window-boxes have disappeared.

Parchment Street
The top end of Parchment Street looking towards High Street shows the Masonic Hall before the conversion of the ground floor into a butcher's shop. For many years a doorway in the middle of the block led to the Awdry Restaurant and Tea Rooms upstairs.

Parchment Street
The former Burton's shop in High Street still dominates the end of Parchment Street but the corner property is now W. H. Smith's. The Awdry Restaurant closed in 1966 and the end of Parchment Street was sealed off to traffic when the pedestrian precinct was created in 1974.

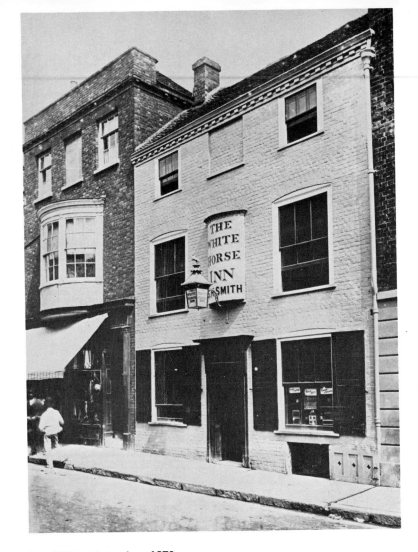

The White Horse Inn, 1879
This old photograph of the White Horse Inn shows the local style of
domestic architecture typical of many Winchester buildings. The shop next
door was an outfitter's and the building to the right of the inn belonged to
the Butt family of shoemakers for four generations.

No. 113 High Street
The White Horse Inn was rebuilt in flint and brick at the end of last century,
with the name worked into the façade. The inn finally lost its licence in 1936.
Hepworths have continued the outfitter's shop and Peter Lord has taken
over from the Butts in selling shoes.

Middle Brook Street, 1935
The camera has captured Marks and Spencer's new building receiving its
finishing touches. St. Maurice's Church replaced an earlier structure in 1842,
and the Victoria Inn was opened by George Eames in 1881. Lewis's barber
shop started in 1897 and was also a boarding house in the 1930s.

17

Middle Brook Street
The three Victorian buildings have been demolished; Harry Lewis's in 1951,
St. Maurice's Church in 1958 and the Victoria Inn in the early 1960s. A
better view of the Cathedral tower can be seen, and the trees planted around
the central car park are an attractive variety of rowan.

High Street braced, 1929
Fleming, Reid and Company's hosiery shop threatened to collapse in 1929 during the building of F. W. Woolworth's store, so bracing was extended across High Street. No. 118 High Street was built as a chapel but was occupied for many years by Gifford's the corn and seed merchants.

High Street pedestrian precinct
Gifford's shop has been incorporated into Woolworth's and the elegant
street frontage fortunately preserved. The pedestrian precinct was created in
February 1974 by stopping traffic access from Market Street junction to St.
Thomas' Street. The precinct was paved with flag-stones in May and June
1976.

Westgate c. 1936
The Westgate is seen flanked by the County Council offices and the Plume of Feathers Inn, complete with mock tower and castellations. The latter replaced an older building last century. The traffic direction signs occupy the site of a drinking fountain which was moved to Oram's Arbour in 1935.

Westgate seen from Upper High Street
The Plume of Feathers was demolished in 1938 exposing the northern side
of the gate. New County Council offices named Elizabeth II Court were
opened in 1959 and include committee rooms. The road now sweeps round
Westgate as modern traffic cannot squeeze through the narrow archway.

Victorian law courts
Law courts were built on to the east end of the Great Hall of Winchester
Castle in 1873. The thirteenth century Great Hall was built on a platform
which falls away steeply towards the city. The law courts were built on
massive foundations which soon began to sink.

Elizabethan law courts
Cracks appeared in the old law courts soon after completion, and the Great
Hall was divided by screens and used as courts. The Victorian building was
finally demolished in 1937 and the site was excavated in the 1960s. New
law courts were built and opened in 1974.

County Police Headquarters, Romsey Road
Hampshire County Police established their first headquarters in this building next to the County Prison which was built 1846–49. Several large institutional buildings were constructed along Romsey Road about this time, and in 1847 the Police Headquarters were situated appropriately close to the prison.

County Police Headquarters, Romsey Road
The modern Police Headquarters were built 1962–65 to designs by
H. Benson Ansell, the then County Architect. The eight-storey building
contains sophisticated equipment to deal with crime detection and
prevention, and a mass of aerials on the roof ensures rapid communication
with all parts of Hampshire.

Royal Hampshire County Hospital
Situated on West Hill opposite the County Gaol in Romsey Road, the
hospital was designed by Butterfield in 1864 from plans drawn up by
Florence Nightingale. Local tradition maintains that Florence Nightingale
chose the site of the hospital, as a hilltop location was considered more
healthy.

Royal Hampshire County Hospital
Winchester was properly drained by sewers in 1878, and immediately the
city became a healthier place. The hospital continued to attract more patients
as its reputation grew in the surrounding countryside. Extensions and
outbuildings were added and a separate maternity unit was opened in 1973.

The Black Swan Hotel
Situated at 65 High Street, the Black Swan Hotel was the terminus for four road waggons which transported heavy goods before the railway was opened in 1838–40. The hotel was run by Charles Sherry in the 1850s but failing to make it pay he opened The Exchange opposite.

Southgate Street

The Black Swan Hotel was demolished in 1934 and the modern block of shops and offices are called Black Swan Buildings. A replica of the inn-sign was carved by Edwin Laverty and adorns the High Street corner. The Exchange has been carried on, as has the newsagent's opposite.

The Green Man, Southgate Street
This early photograph shows the homely Green Man Inn at the junction of
St. Swithun's Street. The tilted stone at the corner protected the brickwork
from damage by carriage wheels. The adjacent terrace of dignified town
houses dates from the early Victorian period.

31

The Green Man, Southgate Street

The Green Man Inn was rebuilt and enlarged in 1881 to become a smart city tavern three storeys high. The name has been worked in stone below the top corner window. Excavations opposite the Green Man in 1971 revealed the Roman south gate of the city.

Christ's Hospital, Symonds Street
This almshouse was founded in 1607 from money bequeathed in 1586 by Peter Symonds, a wealthy Winchester merchant. The endowment provided for six old men, one matron and four boys, and the maintenance of one scholar at Oxford and one at Cambridge.

Christ's Hospital, Symonds Street
The almshouse underwent internal alterations in the 1960s which left the
exterior virtually unchanged. The hospital now accommodates married
couples as well as single men. The founder's name is also remembered in
Peter Symonds' sixth form college, which was a boys' grammar school until
1974.

34

Winchester College
The original buildings of Winchester College date from the late fourteenth century, and the fortress-like appearance of the outer gate is due to the school's situation outside the city wall. The adjacent house is the Warden's Lodging and dates from the sixteenth century.

Winchester College
The outer gate featured in the riots of 1793 and 1818 when the boys
rebelled against the oppressive regime of the Headmaster. On both
occasions the boys barricaded themselves into the school and the Riot Act
was read before peace was restored and the ringleaders expelled.

Back Street, St. Cross
This group of timber framed cottages is a typical example of vernacular
architecture and contrasts with the classical porch of the late eighteenth
century house opposite. Centuries ago the village of St. Cross was know as
Sparkford, and the name is perpetuated in nearby Sparkford Road.

Back Street, St. Cross

The conversion into one residence saw the disappearance of the thatched roof and the introduction of dormer windows. The atmosphere is still charmingly rural although the village is only a mile south of Winchester. St. Cross Hospital can just be seen beyond the trees.

The Heart in Hand, Bar End Road
The Heart in Hand is about two hundred years old, and probably served
refreshments to travellers bound for Portsmouth along the old Roman road
through Morestead and Owslebury. The inn was near the city boundary
when this photograph was taken last century.

The Heart in Hand, Bar End Road
Enlarged if not entirely rebuilt, the modern Heart in Hand stands at the
corner of Milland Road, which was built in 1911 and called New Road until
1927. The large playing field beyond the Heart in Hand is named after King
George V.

The Dog and Duck in the 1930s

The Dog and Duck lost its licence in 1923 and remained empty during the
1930s. The pub had a porch with a simple plank seats where men drank in
fine weather and children played in wet weather. The adjacent dwellings
were near the river and many were damp and unhealthy.

Wharf Hill
Wharf Mill became visible when the Dog and Duck was demolished in 1937.
Wharf Hill was re-developed in the 1960s although the Black Boy on the
extreme left remains. Wharf Mill was grinding corn for SCATS until 1967
and was converted into luxury flats in 1972.

Chesil Street
This photograph was taken before the Didcot, Newbury and Southampton railway was constructed in 1885, as the building next to the Chesil Rectory was demolished to make the station approach. The railway was a Great Western branch line and the station was known locally as Chesil Street Station.

43

Chesil Street
The station approach-road reveals more of the Old Chesil Rectory and The
Cricketers completes the end-street scene. The motor accessories shop used
to be Pointer and Son's brewery in 1895, and the old wagon entrance now
leads to the customers' car park.

City Mill and City Bridge
The City Mill dates from 1744 and is the latest of many mills on the same site. The City Bridge was built of Portland stone in 1813 and spans the river in a single arch. An earlier bridge is reputed to have been built by St. Swithun.

City Mill and City Bridge
The City Mill now belongs to the National Trust and has been used as a
Youth Hostel since 1933. Visitors can appreciate the power of the water
which drove the corn-grinding wheels as the river is forced through the
narrow channels and rushes out under the City Bridge.

The Co-op Bakery, Eastgate Street
The Winchester Co-operative Society first used this building as a bakery in
1933. All the adjacent houses and streets were built on the site of Mildmay
House which was demolished in 1846–47. The Co-op bakery was one of
many industrial buildings in the city.

Greyfriars flats, Eastgate Street
The Co-op bakery was demolished in the early 1960s and the land used for
Council flats. The name Greyfriars was chosen because centuries ago the
land from High Street to Durngate belonged to the Grey Friars. The new
street parallel with Boundary Street is called Friarsgate.

Bibliography

These books are available through Hampshire County Library, and most can be seen at Winchester Library, Jewry Street, Winchester.

Atkinson, T.D. A Survey of the street architecture of Winchester. *Warren, 1934.*

Biddle, M. Winchester in the early Middle Ages; an edition and discussion of the Winton Domesday. *Oxford, Clarendon Press, 1976.*

Carpenter Turner, B.D.M. Winchester, the ancient capital of England. *Pitkin, 1972.*

Green, M. Winchester cavalcade. *Winton Publications, 1965.*

Kitchin, G.W. Winchester (Historic Towns series). *Longmans, Green and Co., 1893.*

Vesey-Fitzgerald, B. Winchester. *Phoenix House, 1953.*

Williamson, H.R. The Ancient capital; an historian in search of Winchester. *Muller, 1953.*

Winchester City Council. Residents' guide to Winchester and district. *British Publishing Co., 1976.*

Winchester College Archaeological Society. Winchester; its history, buildings and people. *Wells, 1921.*